Cornerstones of Freedom

Monticello

Norman Richards

CHILDREN'S PRESS®
A Division of Grolier Publishing
New York • London • Hong Kong • Sydney
Danbury, Connecticut

Library of Congress Cataloging-in-Publication Data

Richards, Norman.
  Monticello / by Norman Richards.
    p. cm.—(Cornerstones of freedom)
  Rev. ed., with new illustrations, of: The story of Monticello, 1970
  Summary: A biography of the farmer, architect, statesman, President,
inventor, and educator whose inventiveness was exemplified by
Monticello.
  ISBN 0-516-06695-1 (lib. bdg.) 0-516-46695-X (pbk.)
  1. Monticello (Va.)—Juvenile literature. 2. Jefferson, Thomas,
1743–1826—Juvenile literature. [1. Monticello (Va.) 2. Jefferson,
Thomas, 1743–1826.] I. Story of Monticello II. Title. III. Series.
E332.74.R5 1995.
975.5'482—dc20   94-35654
                                                              CIP

Thomas Jefferson was born in 1743 and grew up on his family's farm in what is now Albemarle County, Virginia. Across a river from his home was a small, beautiful mountain owned by his father, Peter Jefferson. When Thomas was fourteen years old in 1757, his father died. Thomas inherited the Jefferson land, including the mountain he named "Monticello," which means "little mountain" in Italian.

A view of the Blue Ridge Mountains from Monticello

Thomas Jefferson

As a boy, Thomas liked nothing better than to roam the woods of Monticello, hunting and fishing with his friends. He would climb to the top of the mountain, and he could see for miles in all directions. Someday, Thomas thought, he would build a house of his own on this spot. Indeed, he eventually built a spectacular house there, and Monticello became one of the most famous landmarks in American history.

Thomas Jefferson was a bright and imaginative boy. In school, he studied French, Latin, and Greek, but his interests ranged as wide as

the frontier country in which he was raised.
His curiosity led him to read everything
he could find. When Thomas was seventeen
years old in 1760, he went to the College of
William and Mary in Williamsburg, Virginia.
Williamsburg was a lively city with fine houses
and stores. Sailing ships brought silks from
China and fine furniture from England. Ladies
and gentlemen rode in their carriages dressed in
elegant clothes tailored in London and Paris.

*The College of
William and Mary*

Young Thomas entered into the exciting life of the town. He talked politics with Patrick Henry. He danced at the governor's palace and sometimes played his violin with a group there. He studied law with his mentor, George Wythe, a prominent Virginia attorney. He listened to arguments in the House of Burgesses, the Virginia legislature. He also spent time with Colonel George Washington, who was in charge of the Virginia troops defending the colonial frontier.

Above: George Wythe, Jefferson's mentor in his early years
Right: George Washington as a colonel in the Virginia military

King George III of Great Britain

This was the time of the French and Indian War (1756–1763), the last in a series of wars that had continued since the 1680s. In this war, France and England battled for the rights to territory in northeastern North America. Virginia was a colony owned by Great Britain and was under the rule of King George III. When the war with France ended, England was left with a tremendous debt. King George

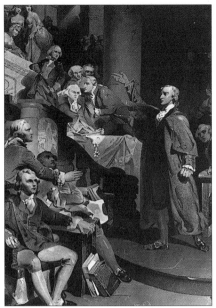

Jefferson witnessed Patrick Henry's famous anti-taxation speech (above), which inspired colonists to protest the British tax laws by burning stamps (right).

decided to raise money by taxing the residents of his American colonies. Great Britain passed the 1765 Stamp Act, which required the colonists to pay extra money to the British government for "stamps"—seals that were required on many kinds of legal documents. The colonists were furious. They believed they should not be taxed because they had no representatives in Parliament to argue their views when the Stamp Act had been passed. The angry colonists protested this "taxation without representation."

Meanwhile, Thomas Jefferson had finished college in 1762. After studying law for several years, he became an attorney in 1767. He was then elected as a representative to the House of Burgesses in 1769. While his busy professional life was based in Williamsburg, Jefferson most enjoyed retreating to his quiet mountain, Monticello, whenever possible. Despite the pressing issues he dealt with in government, Jefferson could not stop thinking about the house he wanted to build on his mountain. In fact, he had already begun planning the house.

Thomas Jefferson was an unusually smart and energetic person. In college, he studied philosophy and mathematics, and for years after college, he studied law. At the same time, he taught himself architecture and designed his Monticello house all by himself!

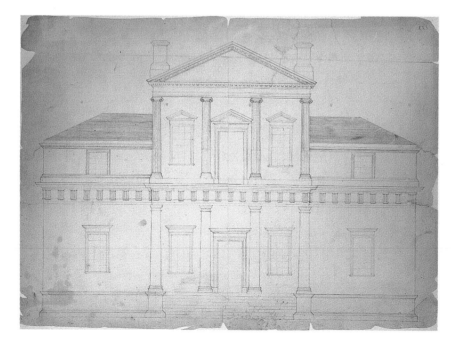

Thomas Jefferson's drawing for the original design of Monticello

The white-columned portico of Monticello's East Front

Before he could start building, however, the top of his mountain had to be leveled. Jefferson made a contract with a worker to clear the land in exchange for payment of 180 bushels of wheat and 24 bushels of corn from Jefferson's plantation. Jefferson was rich in land, but he often had very little cash. In fact, through his life, Jefferson never became a very rich man.

The house Jefferson planned would be different in many ways from the mansions of his friends. Jefferson was intrigued by the classic beauty and simplicity of early Greek and Roman buildings. These influences can be seen in the porticoes with columns that he built at the east and west entrances to his house.

Jefferson planned every detail of the house and spent months collecting the construction materials he needed. He could not easily acquire some materials, such as glass for windows. These, he ordered from England. But much of his building supplies came from his own mountain. Bricks were made from the clay, and lumber was cut from the nearby woods.

Construction of Monticello began in 1769. Jefferson spent many days traveling to the construction site from Williamsburg. He watched his house grow slowly. By the time Jefferson married Martha Wayles Skelton on January 1, 1772, only a few rooms had been completed, yet the young couple moved there in the dead of winter. Their carriage got stuck in a terrible snowstorm, and the newlyweds completed their journey on horseback. The portion of the building in which they lived was once referred to as the "Honeymoon Cottage." It is now called the South Pavilion.

The South Pavilion is the two-story portion of this building. The long connecting building to the right was built later to house Jefferson's slaves.

Jefferson's seven-day clock

As construction continued, word spread throughout Virginia of Jefferson's wonderful house. People came to the mountain and were amazed to see this product of his inventive mind. Jefferson built ingenious wall panels that revolved to reveal handy shelves hidden behind the walls. He put a weather vane on the roof, but its pointer was positioned so it could be seen from inside the house. That way, Jefferson could

Jefferson designed this dumbwaiter to be hidden inside the dining room mantel. It was used to carry bottles of wine from the basement wine cellar to the dining room.

tell the wind direction without going outside. He had a huge clock built that told the day of the week in addition to the time. He also built a special folding ladder to reach the clock when it needed winding. Jefferson even designed tiny dumbwaiters concealed in the side of a fireplace to carry bottles of wine and cider between the dining room and the wine cellar.

The Jefferson family grew as the thirty-five-room house was completed. Thomas and Martha had two little daughters, Martha and Mary. And when Jefferson's sister's husband died, she moved to Monticello with her eight children. Monticello quickly became a happy, lively place. Children laughed and played on the lawn and in the meadows around the house. Jefferson was a kind father to all the youngsters.

Jefferson enjoyed his new home so much that he never wanted to leave. But these were troubled years in the colonies. New British taxes were imposed on the colonists, and tensions between the colonies and Great Britain were growing violent.

War broke out between the British and Americans with major battles at Lexington and Concord,

The fighting at Concord Bridge was one of the battles that marked the beginning of the Revolutionary War.

Massachusetts, in April 1775. As a leader in the Virginia legislature, Jefferson was at the center of the political struggle with Great Britain. He argued that the colonies should declare themselves an independent, free country. It took time, however, before a majority of colonists agreed with him. By July 1776, the need for independence was urgent. Delegates of the

Two events that led to the Revolutionary War were the Boston Massacre (1770) and the Boston Tea Party (1773). In 1770, colonists were angry over the presence of British troops in Boston. A street fight (bottom) got out of control when British troops fired directly into the crowd of colonists (below, left). Three years later, Bostonians protested the British tax on tea by raiding British ships delivering tea to the colonies. They expressed their outrage by dumping the British tea into Boston Harbor (left).

Continental Congress met in Philadelphia that summer and named Jefferson to a committee of five men. The committee's task was to write an official document explaining why the colonies were breaking free from England. This document would be the Declaration of Independence.

Joining Jefferson on the committee were such famous patriots as Benjamin Franklin and John Adams, but Jefferson wrote most of the Declaration on his own. He worked hard for two weeks, writing and rewriting, choosing the proper words. Congress voted to adopt Jefferson's Declaration on July 4, 1776—the date we still celebrate as Independence Day.

With Jefferson's words guiding them, the colonies forged ahead into all-out revolution against Great Britain. King George did not let the colonies go without a fight. He sent more soldiers and ships to North America, and the brutal war lasted seven more years. During the war, Thomas Jefferson served as a member of the Virginia House of Delegates, and he was later elected governor of the state. Jefferson's political career took a blow when British troops stormed through Virginia in 1781. Governor Jefferson was criticized because the state was so poorly defended. After his term as governor ended, Jefferson left office and returned to Monticello. These unhappy times grew much darker when Martha Jefferson died in childbirth in 1782.

As governor, Jefferson spent much of his time at the Governor's Palace in Williamsburg, Virginia.

When the United States finally won the war in 1783, Jefferson returned to public service, hoping to raise his spirits. After serving in Congress, Jefferson spent several years in Paris as the U.S. minister to France. After returning from France, Jefferson began a long period in which he was one of the key figures of the young national government. When George Washington became the nation's first president in 1789, he appointed Thomas Jefferson as his secretary of

Thomas Jefferson (second from left) joins George Washington's cabinet.

state. Jefferson later served as vice president under second president John Adams. And in 1801, Jefferson was elected the country's third president.

Jefferson served two terms as president. While in office, he maintained his faith in the hardworking poor people and continually fought for individuals' rights within the government. Perhaps his most remarkable achievement was the 1803 Louisiana Purchase, in which the United States paid France approximately $15 million for the Louisiana Territory. This purchase expanded the U.S. western frontier from the Mississippi River all the way to the Rocky Mountains.

Just before Jefferson's presidential term began, the U.S. capital was moved to Washington, D.C., and Jefferson was the second president to occupy the White House (which was called the President's House in those days). Jefferson was happy to be living in Washington, which was very close to his beloved home at Monticello. His longing to live full-time at Monticello surely influenced his decision not to run for a third term as president. In 1809, Jefferson decided that after so many years in public service, the time had at last come to retire. Sixty-five-year-old Thomas Jefferson happily left Washington, D.C., and returned permanently to the home he loved.

Thomas Jefferson

Monticello was now a much different place than in previous years. Ever since his return from France, Jefferson had been renovating Monticello, and now it was virtually an entirely new structure. The most noticeable addition was the dome Jefferson added to the roof of the house. Monticello was the first house in America to have a domed roof.

Jefferson also undertook an original approach to expanding the house. Most houses of Jefferson's time consisted of a main house, and clustered around it were a number of "outbuildings"—a laundry, a kitchen, and many other buildings. Jefferson did not like how this cluster of buildings looked. He wanted to make

these service buildings part of the house. So he designed two long terraces that connected these service buildings, which included the cook's room, smokehouse, carriage house, icehouse, and stables. Covered passageways connected these terraces to the main house, making Monticello into a large, U-shaped structure. This way, it was easy to move among the many different parts of the house in any kind of weather.

A view of the two terraces that connect the service buildings to the main house at Monticello.

After all the renovations were finished, Monticello had grown from two stories and thirteen rooms to three stories and forty-three rooms. The house featured dozens of paintings and rare furnishings from all over the world, many of which Jefferson had acquired while in France.

Views of some of Monticello's rooms, including the kitchen (top), the ornate front hall (middle), and Jefferson's study (bottom). On Jefferson's desk is a contraption he used to make a copy of what he was writing.

Some of the interesting objects invented by Jefferson include (clockwise from left): an octagon-shaped table with filing drawers; a special case for bottles of wine and ale that Jefferson took with him on trips away from Monticello; the drafting table on which Jefferson drew the designs for Monticello and many other buildings; and a swivel chair and desk that allowed him to recline and write at the same time.

Monticello was also a fully operating, 5,000-acre plantation on which Jefferson grew wheat, corn, potatoes, and other grains. Jefferson was always experimenting with new crop-growing techniques. In his impressive gardens and orchard he raised many types of plants that were rare to Virginia at the time, including the tulip (from Europe) and the gingko tree (from China).

On the land around Monticello, Jefferson maintained an active plantation.

In his years of retirement, Monticello was filled with the laughter of Jefferson's twelve grandchildren. He took joy in spending time with his grandchildren and planning their daily lessons—they studied nature and French in the morning, took dancing classes in the afternoon, and read in the evening. The children were free to go anywhere on the Monticello grounds, except their grandfather's suite of rooms. In his private bedroom, library, and study, Jefferson preferred to be alone to read and write.

Monticello was home not only to Jefferson and his family, but to dozens of slaves. Slavery in the colonies had been legal under the laws of England, and the United States did not outlaw slavery until 1863. Like all the other landowners in the South, Thomas Jefferson owned slaves and used them not only in working his plantation, but in the building, renovation, and upkeep of Monticello.

Jefferson's slaves were housed below ground level from the main house.

Historians have long attempted to uncover Jefferson's true feelings about slavery. In public debates and in his writings, he appeared violently opposed to the idea. He actually wrote a section of the Declaration of Independence that denounced slavery, but Congress voted to delete it before the Declaration was approved. Jefferson was enraged over this decision. Yet as much as he opposed slavery, there was never a time in his adult life when Jefferson did not own slaves. Some people believe that Jefferson disagreed with the idea of slavery, but he also felt it would be cruel to free his slaves into a society where they would not be able to find employment. So he did his best to house his slaves adequately, treat them humanely, and tend to them when they were sick and grew old. But the fact remained that they were slaves, and even if they were treated well, they were not free to leave Monticello.

Jefferson was not active in politics in his later years, but he was still very active as an architect. He designed homes for many of his friend, and he took on the task of designing buildings for the new University of Virginia at Charlottesville. Since Charlottesville was just a few miles from Monticello, there were days when he could sit on his mountain and watch

the progress of the construction through a telescope. His buildings still stand on the beautiful campus. Jefferson's influence on architectural styles can be seen in many Virginia buildings to this day.

The University of Virginia

The University of Virginia opened at Charlottesville in 1825 with the eighty-two-year-old Jefferson as its first rector. Establishing this university was Jefferson's most treasured project in his old age. He gladly worked hard on this final endeavor because he believed so strongly in the importance of education.

Jefferson once wrote, "All my wishes end where I hope my days will end, at Monticello." He died at Monticello on July 4, 1826—the fiftieth anniversary of the ratification of his Declaration of Independence. Jefferson was buried on the grounds of Monticello, next to his wife.

Today, Monticello is owned by a nonprofit organization, the Thomas Jefferson Memorial Foundation. The house and the grounds are kept in beautiful condition, just as Jefferson, himself, kept them. Visitors travel from all over the world to see this home that was loved so much by one of the founders of the United States. Even today, people marvel at the design of the house and the innovations that Jefferson built into it.

The house called Monticello tells us much about the man who was a farmer, architect, lawyer, author, educator, statesman, president— a genius whose mind was never idle. Thomas Jefferson designed and built a beautiful house that accommodated all the needs of his family. The house remains a marvel of inventiveness to be studied and praised for generations to come.

Statue of Thomas Jefferson

Jefferson's tombstone stands on the grounds at Monticello.

GLOSSARY

Architectural sketch

architecture – the study of how to design and construct buildings

colony – people living in a territory that is ruled by another country or power

Continental Congress – the meetings of representatives from the thirteen colonies during the Revolutionary War; Thomas Jefferson was a delegate to the Second Continental Congress in 1775

delegate – a person authorized to act or speak on behalf of a larger group of citizens

dumbwaiter – a small elevator built into a wall that carries dishes and other supplies from one floor of a house to another

House of Burgesses – a Virginia colonial legislature that was the first body of government in America to be comprised of representatives (the representatives were called "burgesses")

legislature – an assembly of representatives that makes the laws of a community or nation

mason – a worker who builds a structure with bricks or stone

outbuilding – a separate building from the main house, used for storage, work spaces, or as servants' quarters

portico – a covered porch at the entrance of a building

rector – the head of a university or school

renovation – change of the appearance of a house or structure by major construction

Stamp Act – a 1765 law passed by the British Parliament requiring people in all British territories to pay an extra tax on papers that required a government "stamp," or seals

tax – money charged by the government for services or goods

weather vane – a device that shows the direction of the wind

Portico

TIMELINE

Thomas Jefferson born **1743**

1756

French & Indian War

1763

British Stamp Act **1765**

1768 Jefferson begins plans for Monticello

1769 Construction of Monticello begins

1770

1772 Jefferson marries Martha Wayles Skelton

Boston Tea Party **1773**

1775 Revolutionary War begins

1776 Declaration of Independence written

1779

Jefferson serves as governor of Virginia

1781

Martha Jefferson dies **1782**

1783 Revolutionary War ends

U.S. Constitution signed **1787**

1789

Renovation of Monticello begins **1796**

1801

Jefferson's first term as president

1805

Jefferson's second term as president

1809

Boston Massacre

Jefferson is named George Washington's secretary of state

University of Virginia opened **1825**

1826 Jefferson dies at Monticello

INDEX (*Boldface page numbers indicate illustrations.*)

PHOTO CREDITS

Cover, 1, ©Robert C. Lautman Photography; 2, North Wind Picture Archives; 3, Virginia Historical Society; 4, Stock Montage, Inc.; 5, 6 (bottom), North Wind; 6 (top), 7, 8 (left), Bettmann Archive; 8 (right), Stock Montage, Inc.; 9, Courtesy Massachusetts Historical Society; 10, UPI/Bettmann; 11, Photri; 12, Virginia Historical Society; 13, ©Robert C. Lautman Photography; 14, Bettmann; 15 (top and bottom), Stock Montage, Inc.; 15 (left), North Wind; 16, Bettmann; 17, ©Mae Scanlan; 18, North Wind; 20, Bettmann; 21, ©Robert Llewellyn; 22 (top), Photri; 22 (bottom), ©Kevin Fleming; 22 (left), ©Robert C. Lautman Photography; 23 (top right, bottom left, and bottom right), Bettmann; 23 (top left), Library of Congress; 24, 25, ©Robert C. Lautman Photography; 26, Library of Congress; 27, 28, Bettmann; 29 (top), ©Mae Scanlan; 29 (bottom), Monticello/Thomas Jefferson Memorial Foundation, Inc.; 30 (top), Courtesy Massachusetts Historical Society; 30 (bottom), 31 (bottom right), Bettmann; 31 (left), North Wind; 31 (top right), ©Robert C. Lautman Photography

ABOUT THE AUTHOR

Norman Richards grew up in a small New England town and developed an early interest in American history. A graduate of Boston University's School of Journalism, Mr. Richards has written extensively on aviation and travel, and has authored several books in the *Cornerstones of Freedom* series.